W.D.B.©

1

COLOR CLUES
ON
BACK COVER

You would never hurt a **black bear** cub
but the mother doesn't know that.

If you get too close,
she might bite or claw you to protect her young.

2

COLOR CLUES
ON
BACK COVER

Mule deer fawns are kept hidden in the grass by their mother until they learn to sense danger and run from it.

3

COLOR CLUES
ON
BACK COVER

Coyotes are seen sometimes in the early morning as they hunt mice in a Sierra meadow.

Late at night you might hear them howling.

Can you howl like a coyote?

4

COLOR CLUES
ON
BACK COVER

This mother **mountain lion** has her cubs
high on the cliffs for protection.

She may be looking down at some animal
which she will stalk and kill for her cubs' food.

5

COLOR CLUES
ON
BACK COVER

The **raccoon** usually will be seen at night,
as he most often sleeps during daylight.

He eats almost anything but prefers fish, fruits, and acorns.

To escape enemies, he quickly climbs a tree.

6
COLOR CLUES
ON
BACK COVER

A long bushy tail helps us identify the **California gray squirrel.**

These squirrels eat pine seeds and acorns
and will hide them in the ground during the fall
so they will have food for the wintertime.

7

COLOR CLUES
ON
BACK COVER

These two small animals, the **golden-mantled ground squirrel** (top)
and the **chipmunk,** live in dry rocky places.

They dart about quickly in search of seeds and nuts.

The chipmunk has stripes on its face,
the golden-mantled ground squirrel doesn't.

8

COLOR CLUES
ON
BACK COVER

The large strong bill of the **black-headed grosbeak** makes it easy for him to crack and open seeds.

Birds' bills often will tell you the sort of food they eat.

What might the woodpecker's long sharp bill or the eagle's hooked bill tell you about their food?

W. D. B. ©

9
COLOR CLUES
ON
BACK COVER

Mountain quail live among thick brush
where they can find insects and seeds to eat
and for protection, as they are hunted by people and animals.

10

COLOR CLUES
ON
BACK COVER

Nesting high on the cliffs,
the **golden eagle** watches the ground below
for the movement of a rabbit or a mouse
which would make a fine meal for her young.

11

COLOR CLUES
ON
BACK COVER

The male **Western tanager's** brightly colored feathers
help him attract a female, whose colors are drab;
in nature, males usually are more colorful than females.

12

COLOR CLUES
ON
BACK COVER

The noisy **Steller's jay** will invite himself to your picnic
and will squawk his demand for a bite, but don't feed him.

There is plenty of his natural food around,
and seeds and insects are much better for him than people-food.

13

COLOR CLUES
ON
BACK COVER

Don't harm this brilliantly colored snake;
he is a **California mountain king snake.**

You can't mistake the vivid red, white, and black
bands that go around his body.

Sometimes people kill this snake,
confusing it with the poisonous coral snake,
which doesn't live in this region.

14

COLOR CLUES
ON
BACK COVER

Although the **alligator lizard** looks like a ferocious miniature of his namesake, he is quite harmless.

You shouldn't handle him, though, as he may give your finger a hard pinch in his jaws.

15

COLOR CLUES
ON
BACK COVER

When the brown and gray **rattlesnake** shakes his tail,
get out of his way!

Keep a sharp eye on the trail ahead and you'll avoid danger,
as he will only strike at you if you frighten or surprise him.

He prefers mice!

16

These three amphibians might look quite similar.

However, the one on the tree branch is a **Pacific tree-frog,**
at the bottom a **California yellow-legged frog,**
and the one on the right a **Yosemite toad.**

The Yosemite toad is found almost exclusively in Yosemite.

The others are found all through the Sierra.